Waiting for the Next Crisis
A Memoir

Vexing and Poignant Moments

with my

90 Year Old Mother

N. Scrantz Lersch

For permission contact:

Scrantz

Studio 37
Portland, Oregon
Madison, Wisconsin
USA
at
scrantz@gmail.com

Waiting for the Next Crisis - A Memoir/ Vexing and Poignant Moments with my 90 Year Old Mother
1. Memoir 2. Mothers and daughters 3. Suicide attempt 4. Elderly mothers
5. Therapy for Seniors 6. Parent child 7. Cartoon therapy
8. End of life questions 9. Graphic novel

Studio 37 Publications
502 Leonard Street, Madison, Wisconsin 53711

ISBN-13 : 978-0615731667
ISBN-10 : 061573166X

For

Bob, Julie and Jack

Dedicated to the caregivers.

Try to laugh.

Get help if you need it.

My mother and I loved each other.
We had many things in common.
We loved our artistic pursuits, gardening, reading,
and keeping in touch with old friends.

We loved animals, especially cats.
We would rather sit at home in worn clothes
and watch a sunset, than go shopping.

We lived 300 miles from each other.
As her health deteriorated, it became harder
and harder to solve her problems and arrange help.
She often said crazy and illogical things
that were hurtful and confusing.
I began to draw cartoons of our conversations,
to make sense of them.
I also drew them to make myself laugh.
I wanted to remind myself that while Life is painful,
it can also be absurd and funny.

Anti
CRAZY MOTHER CREAM

❧

Apply early and often!
Guaranteed to make
all of your mother's
hurtful and absurd
comments slide off.

Leaves no residue!

❧

Use with our
CALMING CREAM
for maximum benefits.

NEW FORMULA!

CALMING CREAM

❧

Apply early and often!
Guaranteed to produce
a calm and pleasant
demeanor.

❧

Use with our
other great products
for maximum benefits.

4

5

My elderly mother needed lots of help....

Gerontologist for primary care and prescriptions
Orthopedic surgeon for hips, knee and shoulder replacements
Gero-psychologist for depression and suicidal tendencies
Rheumatologist for joints and steroid injections
Psychiatric RN for home visits for depression
Dermatologist for skin rashes and keratoses
Cardiac surgeon for heart valve replacement
Physical therapist for recovery from surgeries
Dentist for teeth and crowns
Optometrist for glasses
Eye surgeon for cataracts
Cardiologist for heart
Hearing aid specialist
Hairdresser for perms and haircuts
Podiatrist for toenail cutting
Phlebotomist for blood draws and INR monitoring
Radiologist for mammograms and CAT scans after falls

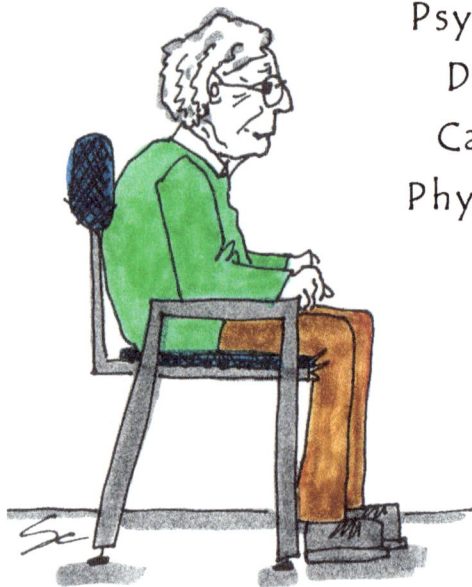

You BROKE MY HEART when you left home at 17. I wanted a child for so long and tried so hard. And after my heart surgery you left me. ** You said you had your own life.

? ? ?

** with a 24-hour a day caregiver

My mother hated getting old.
She hated asking for help
or feeling "beholden" to anyone.
She often felt misunderstood.

9

My husband was a voice of reason....

We got along fine until you were about six or seven.... Well – I couldn't just TALK to you....

HOLD ON! STOP! People pay a lot of money to psychoanalysts to have this conversation. We are NOT having it now!

Can she say ANYTHING more Ridiculous ??

Huh? Are you saying we didn't get along after I was six or seven?

We lived from crisis to crisis
until we found her an apartment
in a continuing care community
just five miles from our house.

THE
NEXT
CRISIS

The DEMANDS

Honey, I don't want a birthday party.
Let's have one in October, or August,
Or Never.

I want a subscription to the N.Y. Times.
Sign me up...
And I need some things.
I'll get you my list.

Sunday, at my house......

Honey, can I have this bottle of lotion?

You can buy yourself another one and that can be your birthday present.

Umm, sure...

The next week – at her apartment....

Gee, YOU sure got
the Better Deal.
I get one inch of lotion,
and you get a
brand new bottle!

15

You made me buy new hearing aids.
You made me spend $8000 **
And now I'm OUT OF MONEY!

You can force me to BUY them,
But you can't force me
To WEAR THEM!

** aids cost = $ 4000

Hi Mom!
Your birthday is tomorrow,
would you like me to
come over for lunch?

I could come over after
that and we could get a
box lunch and eat together.

I am NOT busy tomorrow!
I had planned to have
Lunch with YOU!

NO! I have that
physical therapy
person coming.
I can't go to lunch.

Oh NO,
you're busy.

19

20

We went to museums and out to lunch.

LOOK at this serving! Who do they think is coming? The THIRD BATTALION?

You can take the leftovers home.

I made all of my mother's appointments and escorted her to them.
I typed up "reminder notes" after each doctor visit.
I ordered all of her meds and filled her "daily med" boxes every month.
But I could NOT give her the ONE thing she wanted.
She wanted to be young again. She hated being old.

My mother suffered from depression.
She had lost her husband of 44 years
and her best friends. She was sad.
Who wouldn't be?
She couldn't drive anymore
and she tired easily.
In spite of the new digital hearing aids,
even talking on the phone was difficult.

I found a wonderful, sympathetic geropsychologist.
After four visits, my mother was not interested
in talking to her anymore. My mother was from the
"Just pull yourself up by your bootstraps!"
and "Grin and bear it" generation.

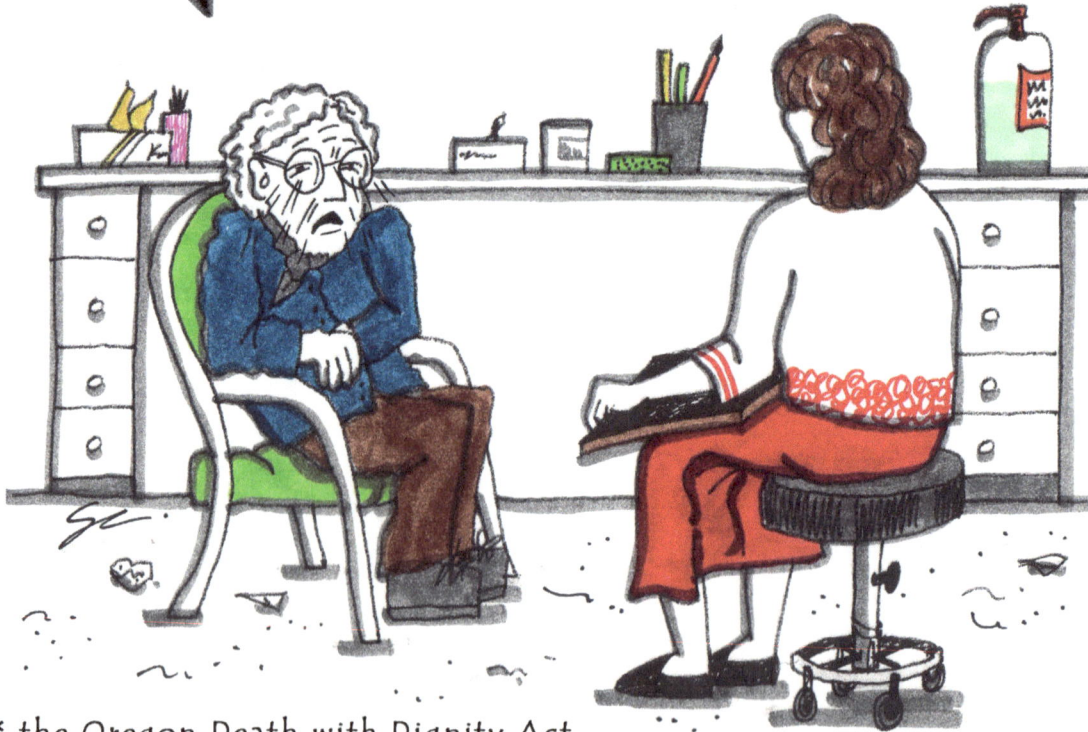

** the Oregon Death with Dignity Act.

And then there was
The Suicide Attempt.
It was NOT funny.

2:17 AM

....the hospital calling...

Her suicide attempt was unsuccessful
and I was left with some heavy baggage.

The WORRY MONSTER came almost every night.
I was terrified that my mother would lose her apartment.

30

I was fortunate to have an excellent psychologist.
My doctor was able to give me the tools
I needed to survive this emotional crisis.
It was a difficult time.

After my mother got out of the hospital,
she returned to her apartment.
She came to her granddaughter's wedding
and had a wonderful time.

She needed daily help and that fall we moved her
to an apartment with a view of birds and flowers,
in the assisted living wing of her community.

My mother did not like needing help to bathe or cook meals.
She did not like being dependent on anyone in any way.
She suffered from congestive heart failure
and needed oxygen during her last months.

Finally, her doctor admitted her to hospice.

My mother died at age 93.
I was holding her hand.
We scattered her ashes in a beautiful creek,
deep in the forest on a hot summer day.

Peggy Perkins Lersch
1915 - 2008

Clockwise from top left:

1954 - My mother and me
2005 - My mother on New Year's Eve
1971 - My mother, my father and me

Acknowledgments

All of the scenes illustrated in this book really happened.
I drew them when they occurred and kept them in a folder.
Two years after my mother died, I was moved to redraw the cartoons
and collect them in a book. My hope is that the millions of people
caring for their elderly parents will feel less alone after reading this book.

To Art Spiegelman and Lynda Barry, thanks for the inspiration.

To Dr. G. - Thank you.

To my children, Julie and Jack, who hugged me and helped me believe that
I was not the crazy one! Thank you. I will try to be a nice old lady!

Finally, thanks to my brilliant husband, Bob Shapiro,
who held me during the tough nights and days and kept me laughing.
Everything I am today is due to your love and support.

www.ingramcontent.com/pod-product-compliance
Lightning Source LLC
Chambersburg PA
CBHW041547040426
42447CB00002B/83